Why your company shouldn't consider communication as an expense: strategies that prove that good communication brings returns

Copyright © 2024 Reginaldo Osnildo
All rights reserved.

PRESENTATION

INTRODUCTION TO COMMUNICATION AS INVESTMENT

THE VALUE OF BRANDING

CONTENT STRATEGIES THAT ENGAGE

VISUAL COMMUNICATION AND ITS INFLUENCE

THE POWER OF STORYTELLING

INFLUENCER MARKETING: PROVEN ROI

SEO: A LONG-TERM STRATEGY

INTERNAL COMMUNICATION AND TEAM ENGAGEMENT

DIGITAL PUBLIC RELATIONS

EMAIL MARKETING: CONVERSIONS AND RELATIONSHIP

CRISIS MANAGEMENT AND ONLINE REPUTATION

CUSTOMER FEEDBACK AS A STRATEGIC TOOL

MULTIPLATFORM COMMUNICATION STRATEGIES

DATA ANALYSIS FOR DECISION MAKING

CORPORATE SOCIAL RESPONSIBILITY

CORPORATE EVENTS AND PRODUCT LAUNCHES

INVESTMENT IN COMMUNICATION TECHNOLOGY

NETWORKING AND STRATEGIC PARTNERSHIPS

MULTICULTURAL AND GLOBAL COMMUNICATION

PAID ADVERTISING: EVALUATING ROI

NONVERBAL COMMUNICATION AND ITS IMPORTANCE

THE PODCAST ERA: HAVING ADVANTAGE OF NEW CHANNELS

SUSTAINABILITY IN COMMUNICATION

MEASURING THE IMPACT OF COMMUNICATION

REGINALDO OSNILDO

PRESENTATION

You are about to embark on a transformative journey through the world of corporate communication, where each word, image and strategy are not seen as mere costs, but as powerful investments, capable of leveraging brands, engaging customers and significantly boosting financial results.

This book was meticulously crafted with you in mind, as a business leader, marketing or communications professional, who seeks not only to understand the essence of effective communication but also to apply it in a practical and up-to-date way for today. Here, you will find a complete guide, packed with proven strategies, innovative insights and practical tips to transform communication from a perceived cost into a valuable asset for your business.

WHY IS THIS BOOK AN ESSENTIAL RESOURCE?

We live in an era where information is abundant, but attention is scarce. In this context, the ability to communicate effectively becomes an invaluable competitive advantage. Through the pages of this book, you will be guided through the deconstruction of old myths and the construction of a new perception about communication — a perception where each communicative action is a strategic investment in brand building, customer engagement and sustainable business growth.

WHAT CAN YOU EXPECT WHEN YOU TURN EACH PAGE?

You will be introduced to revolutionary concepts and up-to-date techniques that cover everything from the importance of branding to the power of digital communication across multiple platforms, the art of storytelling, SEO strategies, influencer marketing, crisis management, and much more. In addition, this book is peppered with real-life success stories, demonstrating how companies from various sectors have transformed their communication into a powerful tool to conquer markets and captivate hearts.

A JOURNEY THAT STARTS WITH YOU

Each chapter of this book is designed to be complete in itself, but also to connect to the next, ensuring a fluid and engaging reading experience . And, at the end of each chapter, you will be invited to take another step on this journey, exploring new dimensions of business communication that can be immediately applied to your context.

This is more than a book; it is an invitation for you, the reader, to delve into the depths of communication as a strategic investment, capable of transforming the reality of your business. Together, we will update communication concepts for today, making their application not only more effective, but also simpler and more direct.

Are you ready to transform your company's communication into a pillar of growth and success?

Let's go ahead and discover how each strategy, each message and each channel can be optimized to take your brand and results to levels never before achieved.

As we move forward, remember that every insight and tactic presented here is the result of in-depth analysis and adaptation to new market realities. This book is a reflection of my commitment to synthesizing advanced communication knowledge and transforming it into accessible and applicable strategies that will facilitate your journey to success.

With that goal in mind, I invite you to begin this journey with me. Dive in, explore each chapter, and most importantly, apply what you learn. This is not just a theoretical guide; it is a practical roadmap for the transformation you want to see in your organization.

As we explore together the many facets of corporate communications, from creating memorable branding to crisis management and online reputation, you will discover the undeniable power of well-planned and executed communications. And by the end of this journey, I hope you will not only see communications as a valuable investment, but also as a key strategic differentiator for the sustainable growth and longevity of your business in today's competitive marketplace.

The next chapter, **"INTRODUCTION TO COMMUNICATION AS AN INVESTMENT"** , will open the doors to this new understanding, deconstructing the myth of communication as a cost and redefining it as a crucial investment in business success. Prepare to have your perceptions challenged and your vision expanded.

So, are you ready to take the first step on this exciting journey? The transformation begins now, and all you need to do is turn the page.

Welcome to the future of business communication. Welcome to the starting point for exponential growth for your business. Together, we will transform communication from a perceived cost into a valuable and undeniable investment.

Your journey to excellence in business communications starts here.

Yours sincerely

Reginaldo Osnildo

INTRODUCTION TO COMMUNICATION AS AN INVESTMENT

Dear reader, have you ever wondered why, in many organizations, communication is often seen as an expense rather than a strategic investment? This perception can be the biggest obstacle to business growth and innovation. In this chapter, we will debunk this myth and redefine communication as the essential investment that it truly is for the success of any business.

COMMUNICATION: COST OR INVESTMENT?

Historically, communications has been pigeonholed into corporate expense spreadsheets, a narrow view that obscures its true value. But when executed strategically, communications transcends this narrow view to act as an engine for customer engagement, brand building, and ultimately, sustainable financial returns. The first step is to shift our mindset from a reactive stance to a proactive and strategic approach to communications.

COMMUNICATION AS A LEVER OF VALUE

As a business leader, marketing or communications professional, you should see each message, campaign or content as an opportunity to add value to your brand and connect meaningfully with your audience. Instead of asking how much a communications strategy will cost, ask yourself what value it can add to your business in the medium and long term.

BUILDING STRONG BRANDS AND LASTING RELATIONSHIPS

A strong brand is not built overnight, nor is it by chance. It is the result of consistent, creative, and engaging communication that resonates with your audience. This chapter will guide you through strategies for using communication not only to inform, but to delight and create an emotional connection with your audience. Customer loyalty and brand differentiation in the marketplace are direct results of smart investments in communication.

MEASURING IMPACT AND RETURN ON INVESTMENT (ROI)

One of the biggest advantages of strategic communication is its ability to be measured. Unlike many other business investments, the impact of communication can be quantified through a variety of metrics, such as engagement, reach, conversions and, of course, financial return.

Companies that recognize and capitalize on communication as a strategic investment are better positioned to stand out from the competition, adapt to market changes and cultivate strong relationships with their customers.

This chapter has challenged the traditional perception of communication as a cost, highlighting its fundamental role as a strategic investment in business growth and success. But how can we build a brand that truly stands out in the marketplace and in the minds of consumers?

In the next chapter, **"THE VALUE OF BRANDING ,"** we'll dive into the world of effective branding. We'll explore how targeted, authentic communication can not only differentiate your brand in the marketplace, but also create a perception of invaluable value in the minds of your consumers.

THE VALUE OF BRANDING

Welcome to the chapter that could redefine the way you view your brand and its impact on the business world. Branding isn't just about a flashy logo or catchy slogan; it's about building a brand essence that resonates deeply with your customers and sets you apart in a crowded marketplace. Here, we'll explore how effective branding is, in fact, an invaluable investment in your business's future.

THE ESSENCE OF BRANDING

Branding is the art of creating and managing your brand identity, cultivating a unique image and value promise that resonates in the minds of your audience. When done correctly, branding transcends the product or service itself, evoking emotions and creating bonds of loyalty that outlast the inevitable market fluctuations.

WHY INVEST IN BRANDING?

An investment in branding is an investment in the perceived value of your brand. This perception directly influences consumers' purchasing decisions, allowing you to command premium prices, attract ideal customers, and create barriers to entry against competitors. In a world where consumers are bombarded with choices, a strong brand is your best ally to stand out and capture the attention of your target audience.

BUILDING DIFFERENTIATION IN THE MARKET

At the heart of effective branding is differentiation. Whether it's through a unique value proposition, a compelling brand story, or an unforgettable customer experience, the goal is to create something that no one else offers. We'll discuss practical strategies for discovering and communicating what makes your brand unique, creating a market position that's both distinctive and desirable.

THE JOURNEY TO CUSTOMER LOYALTY

Customer loyalty is the holy grail for any business, and branding is the way to achieve it. By creating a brand that customers love and trust, you not only ensure their repeat business, but you also turn customers into true brand ambassadors. We'll explore how ongoing investment in branding can cultivate this loyalty, turning transactions into lasting relationships.

The true value of branding often transcends direct measurement, lying in increased perception of value, customer loyalty, and engagement. However, there are metrics and indicators that can help you assess the impact of your branding, from brand awareness to market share.

The brands that will remain relevant will be those that not only communicate a promise of value, but also consistently deliver on that promise through every customer interaction and experience.

This chapter has highlighted branding not as a cost, but as a crucial investment in differentiating yourself and building a lasting legacy. By investing in branding, you are investing in the foundation upon which your company can grow, innovate, and thrive.

In the next chapter, **"CONTENT STRATEGIES THAT ENGAGE ,"** we'll explore how to develop relevant content that not only captures your audience's attention but also fosters deep and lasting loyalty. Get ready to learn the art of storytelling that resonates, engages, and converts.

CONTENT STRATEGIES THAT ENGAGE

As we delve into the heart of effective communication, we come to a fundamental element: content. This chapter is not just about creating content, but about forging deep, lasting connections with your audience through messages that resonate, engage, and inspire. Here, you'll learn how to harness the power of content to not only capture attention, but also cultivate loyalty and drive action.

THE POWER OF RELEVANT CONTENT

In a world flooded with information, the challenge is not simply to be heard, but to be remembered. Relevant content is content that speaks to the needs, wants, and interests of your audience, providing value in every word. Let's explore how understanding your audience deeply can lead to the creation of content that not only engages, but also establishes your brand as a trusted authority in your industry.

STRATEGIES FOR DEVELOPING CONTENT THAT SPEAKS TO THE HEART

The most powerful content is that which touches the emotions, creating an emotional resonance that transcends convention. We will learn the art of storytelling that captures the imagination and fosters an emotional connection, transforming passive viewers into active participants and ambassadors for your brand.

ENGAGEMENT THROUGH PERSONALIZATION

The digital age has brought with it the expectation of personalization. Your audience wants to feel like every message was crafted with them in mind. We'll discuss how personalization can be applied to your content strategies, from precise segmentation to message customization, to increase engagement and relevance for each individual.

OPTIMIZING CONTENT FOR ACTION

Every piece of content should have a clear purpose, whether it's to inform, entertain, inspire or convert. Here, we'll outline how to create effective calls to action (CTAs) that direct your readers to the next step, whether that's making a purchase, signing up for a newsletter or sharing on social media, turning engagement into tangible action.

As with any other form of investment in communication, it is crucial to measure the impact of your content.

The key to standing out will be the ability to evolve, experiment and adapt to changing audience preferences and market trends, while always remaining relevant and engaging .

In this chapter, we unlock the transformative potential of relevant, engaging content . We see how carefully planned strategies can create not just interest, but a lasting connection that fosters loyalty and drives action.

As you continue on this journey, I invite you to explore the next chapter, **"VISUAL COMMUNICATION AND ITS INFLUENCE ,"** where we will dive into the impact of visual communication on brand perception and consumer preference. Get ready to discover how to use visual elements to reinforce your message and capture the essence of your brand in a powerful and memorable way.

VISUAL COMMUNICATION AND ITS INFLUENCE

In the world of marketing and corporate communication, images speak as loudly as words. In this chapter, we will explore the vast territory of visual communication, an essential component for capturing attention, evoking emotions and strengthening your brand identity. Here, you will discover how to use visual elements not only to complement your verbal message, but to communicate more directly and impactfully with your audience.

THE IMPACT OF VISUAL COMMUNICATION

In an age dominated by visual culture, first impressions are often visual. From your website design to your social media posts, every visual aspect of your brand contributes to the narrative you want to tell. Let's dive into the principles of effective design and how they can be applied to create coherent, compelling visual communication that sets your brand apart.

CREATING A STRIKING VISUAL IDENTITY

A strong visual identity is crucial to market differentiation. Elements such as logos, color palettes, and typography work together to create an image that is instantly recognizable and memorable to consumers. This chapter will provide insights into how to develop and maintain a visual identity that reflects your brand's values and essence, creating an instant connection with your audience.

PHOTOGRAPHY AND VIDEO: VISUAL STORYTELLING THAT ENGAGES

At the heart of effective visual communication are photography and video, powerful storytelling tools that can convey your message in a dynamic and engaging way. We'll discuss how to use these mediums to tell your brand story, showcase your products or services, and connect emotionally with your audience, increasing engagement and retention.

THE IMPORTANCE OF VISUAL CONSISTENCY

Visual consistency across all platforms and touchpoints is key to building trust and brand recognition. We'll cover strategies to ensure your visual communication is seamless and coherent, reinforcing your brand identity and making it easier for your audience to remember.

Just like any other aspect of communication, the effectiveness of your visual strategy needs to be measured.

Visual communication will continue to evolve, with new technologies and trends shaping the way brands communicate visually. Staying up to date and adapting to new tools and platforms will be essential to maintaining the relevance and impact of your visual communication.

This chapter has illuminated the critical role of visual communication in building a strong brand and creating an emotional connection with your audience. Through a cohesive and impactful visual strategy, you can communicate the essence of your brand more effectively and memorably.

Now, get ready to enter the world of storytelling in the next chapter, **"THE POWER OF STORYTELLING"** . We will discover how stories can be used to communicate brand values, missions and differentiators in a way that resonates deeply with your audience, creating a brand that is not only recognized, but loved.

THE POWER OF STORYTELLING

On our journey to transform communication from a perceived cost to an invaluable investment, we come to one of the most powerful elements of human communication: storytelling. This chapter explores how engaging narratives can not only convey the essence of your brand, but also create lasting emotional connections with your audience. Through storytelling, you can inspire, engage, and motivate in unique ways, leaving an indelible mark on your customers' memories.

THE POWER OF STORIES IN BRAND COMMUNICATION

Stories have the power to capture our attention, evoke emotions, and make us more memorable. In a business context, storytelling can transform basic information about products or services into captivating narratives that resonate on a personal level with your audience. We'll explore how to use stories to illustrate your brand values, highlight your market differentiation, and create a cohesive brand experience.

ELEMENTS OF EFFECTIVE STORYTELLING

For a story to be effective, it must have certain elements: an engaging plot, relatable characters, a conflict or challenge, and a satisfying resolution. In this segment, we'll discuss how to build these elements in a way that aligns with your brand message and your audience's interests, creating stories that are not only heard, but felt and remembered.

APPLYING STORYTELLING ACROSS DIFFERENT PLATFORMS

Storytelling isn't limited to a single format or channel; it can be expressed through text, images, videos, and even podcasts. Here, we'll look at how to adapt your stories to different platforms, maintaining the essence of your message while maximizing engagement by personalizing content to meet your audience's expectations and consumption habits.

MEASURING THE IMPACT OF STORYTELLING

Measuring storytelling success goes beyond conventional metrics. In this chapter, we'll cover how to measure the emotional impact and resonance of your stories, using direct audience feedback, engagement analytics, and other qualitative metrics that can provide valuable insights into the effectiveness of your narratives.

In addition to attracting new customers, storytelling is a powerful loyalty tool. Stories that reflect common experiences or illustrate the positive impact your brand has on people's lives can strengthen customer loyalty, turning consumers into brand advocates and ambassadors.

Brands that can tell their stories in an authentic and emotionally engaging way will continue to capture hearts and minds, regardless of changes in consumer trends or communication technologies.

In this chapter, we explore how storytelling is essential to creating a brand that not only communicates, but truly connects with its audience. The stories we tell have the power to transform perception, engage emotionally, and build deep loyalty.

Get ready now to enter the world of **"INFLUENCER MARKETING: PROVEN ROI"** . In this next chapter, we will discover how the power of influencers can be leveraged to expand your brand's reach, build trust and ultimately drive tangible results for your business.

INFLUENCER MARKETING: PROVEN ROI

We now turn to a strategy that has reshaped the rules of engagement and brand promotion: influencer marketing. This chapter will explore how this powerful tool can not only amplify the reach of your message, but also strengthen consumer trust in your brand. In a world where authenticity is highly valued, influencers offer a direct path to connecting with audiences in a meaningful way with proven return on investment (ROI).

WHAT IS INFLUENCER MARKETING?

Influencer marketing involves collaborating with individuals who have an engaged following on social media platforms to promote products, services, or a brand as a whole. These influencers can range from celebrities to niche experts, each with the ability to affect their audience's purchasing decisions due to their authority, knowledge, position, or relationship with their audience.

CHOOSING THE RIGHT INFLUENCER

Success in influencer marketing starts with carefully selecting influencers who align with your brand values and image. We'll discuss how to identify potential partners who not only have a large following, but also have high engagement rates and an audience that overlaps with your target audience.

BUILDING AUTHENTIC RELATIONSHIPS

The key to an effective influencer marketing campaign is authenticity. We'll cover strategies for building genuine relationships with influencers, ensuring that promotions feel natural and resonate with audiences. This includes allowing influencers creative freedom in how they present your brand, while staying true to their own style and voice.

MEASURING INFLUENCER MARKETING ROI

Measuring the success of influencer marketing goes beyond counting likes and followers. In this chapter, we'll look at how to measure the true ROI of these campaigns, looking at metrics like reach, engagement, website traffic, and conversions. We'll also discuss the role of technologies and tools available to track and analyze the performance of your initiatives.

Despite its many advantages, influencer marketing is not without its challenges. Brands that adapt and innovate in this area will maintain a competitive advantage.

This chapter revealed how influencer marketing can be a powerful strategy for expanding your brand's reach, building trust, and generating significant ROI. Through strategic partnerships with influencers, your brand can reach new audiences in an authentic and impactful way.

Get ready now to dive into the world of **"SEO: A LONG-TERM STRATEGY"** . In the next chapter, we will explore how optimizing your online presence for search engines can not only increase your visibility, but also contribute to sustainable long-term organic growth.

SEO: A LONG-TERM STRATEGY

Digging deeper into the essential strategies to boost your brand's growth and visibility, we come to the territory of SEO (Search Engine Optimization). Engine Optimization or Search Engine Optimization). This chapter reveals how a well-planned and executed SEO approach is not just a digital marketing strategy, but a fundamental investment that ensures organic and sustainable growth in the long term.

UNDERSTANDING SEO

SEO is the process of optimizing your website and online content to improve your ranking in search engine results, such as Google. A higher ranking translates into greater visibility to your target audience, resulting in more organic traffic to your website. We'll explore the basics of SEO, from keyword research to on-page and off -page optimization , and how they contribute to your brand's online visibility.

WHY IS SEO A LONG-TERM INVESTMENT?

Unlike quick-response marketing strategies like paid advertising, SEO takes time and patience to produce results. However, once it gains traction, SEO can generate a steady and sustainable flow of high-quality traffic. We'll discuss the importance of viewing SEO as a long-term investment and how it can provide a significant ROI over time.

SEO STRATEGIES FOR SUSTAINABLE GROWTH

In this segment, we'll dive into specific SEO strategies that can help ensure organic growth for your business. We'll cover advanced optimization techniques, quality link building, local SEO for regional businesses, and how mobile optimization has become indispensable in today's digital age.

CHALLENGES AND HOW TO OVERCOME THEM

The road to SEO success is fraught with challenges, from ever-evolving search engine algorithms to intense keyword competition. Let's discuss the most common obstacles brands face on their SEO journeys and effective strategies to overcome them, ensuring your brand not only survives but thrives in the digital space.

Measuring the impact of your SEO strategies is crucial to understanding your success and areas that require adjustments.

This chapter has highlighted SEO as an essential long-term strategy for any brand looking to increase its online visibility and ensure sustainable organic growth. With the right approach, patience, and perseverance, SEO can significantly transform your brand's digital presence.

Get ready now to enter the world of **"INTERNAL COMMUNICATION AND TEAM ENGAGEMENT"**. In the next chapter, we will explore the vital importance of effective communication within your organization and how it can boost productivity and employee satisfaction, crucial elements for the long-term success of any business.

INTERNAL COMMUNICATION AND TEAM ENGAGEMENT

As we continue our journey to transform communication into a strategic investment, we turn our attention to an often underestimated but crucial aspect: internal communication. This chapter is dedicated to exploring how effective internal communication can be the backbone of a motivated, productive and engaged team, forming the basis for the sustainable success of any organization.

THE IMPORTANCE OF INTERNAL COMMUNICATION

Internal communication goes beyond simply sharing operational information. It is essential to building a positive organizational culture, aligning employees with company goals, and creating a sense of belonging. We will discuss how a well-planned internal communication strategy can increase employee satisfaction, reduce turnover, and boost productivity.

STRATEGIES TO IMPROVE TEAM ENGAGEMENT

In this segment, we'll cover practical tactics for engaging your team through communication. These include implementing effective communication platforms, developing two-way feedback programs, celebrating successes, and being transparent about challenges. We'll explore how these strategies can be applied to empower your team and improve overall company performance.

OVERCOMING BARRIERS TO EFFECTIVE COMMUNICATION

Internal communications can face a variety of obstacles, from resistance to change to a lack of resources or inadequate tools. We'll examine common internal communications challenges and offer solutions to overcome them, ensuring your message is heard and understood by your entire team, regardless of the size or geographic distribution of your organization.

TOOLS AND TECHNOLOGIES FOR INTERNAL COMMUNICATION

Technology plays a key role in facilitating effective internal communication. We'll look at the most effective tools and platforms on the market, from intranet systems to messaging apps and collaboration platforms. We'll also discuss how to select and implement these technologies to meet your team's specific needs.

Evaluating the success of your internal communication strategies is essential to understanding what works and what needs to be adjusted.

This chapter has highlighted the vital importance of internal communication in creating a positive organizational culture and boosting employee productivity and satisfaction. Investing in internal communication is investing in the people who drive your company, laying the foundation for external success.

Get ready to explore the world of **"DIGITAL PUBLIC RELATIONS"** in the next chapter. We'll discover how digital PR can be a powerful tool for shaping public perception of your brand, building media relationships, and effectively managing your online reputation.

DIGITAL PUBLIC RELATIONS

As we continue our journey to transform communications into a valuable investment, we turn our attention to a crucial element in building brand image: Digital Public Relations (Digital PR). In this chapter, we will explore how digital PR can be a powerful lever for shaping public perception of your brand, establishing credibility, and proactively managing your online reputation.

WHAT IS DIGITAL PUBLIC RELATIONS?

Digital PR combines traditional PR techniques with online strategies to increase a brand's online presence. This includes working with online content, digital influencers, SEO, and social media to create positive narratives around your brand. Let's discuss how digital PR differs from traditional PR and why it's essential in the digital age.

EFFECTIVE DIGITAL PR STRATEGIES

This segment delves into key digital PR strategies, from developing content that resonates with your audience to building strong relationships with digital influencers and journalists. We'll explore techniques for creating and distributing online press releases, optimizing content for SEO, and utilizing social media to amplify the reach of your message.

ONLINE REPUTATION MANAGEMENT

Your brand's online reputation has never been more important than it is now. We'll cover proactive methods of reputation management, including monitoring brand mentions, responding to online criticism, and crisis management. We'll discuss how a solid digital PR strategy can help prevent reputational damage and how to respond effectively if your brand faces a public challenge.

MEASURING DIGITAL PR SUCCESS

Evaluating the impact of your digital PR initiatives is crucial to understanding their effectiveness and adjusting strategies as needed. We'll explore the most relevant metrics and tools for measuring digital PR success, including analyzing media coverage, social media engagement, website traffic, and conversions attributed to PR efforts.

While digital PR offers many opportunities, it also comes with its own set of challenges.

This chapter highlighted how digital public relations is essential to building and maintaining your brand image in the online world. By leveraging digital PR strategies, you can significantly improve public perception of your brand, establish credibility, and proactively manage your online reputation.

Get ready now to enter the realm of **"EMAIL MARKETING: CONVERSIONS AND RELATIONSHIPS"** in the next chapter. We will explore how to use email marketing to not only drive sales and conversions, but also to build and nurture lasting relationships with your customers.

EMAIL MARKETING: CONVERSIONS AND RELATIONSHIPS

As we continue our journey to transform communication into a valuable investment, we delve into the world of email marketing. This chapter aims to uncover how this classic digital marketing tool continues to be one of the most effective for boosting conversions while also building deep, lasting relationships with your audience.

WHY EMAIL MARKETING?

Email marketing provides a direct and personal route to your customers' inboxes, allowing for targeted and personalized communications that are hard to match on other platforms. Let's explore the statistics that support the effectiveness of email marketing and why it should be a central part of your digital communications strategy.

BUILDING A QUALITY EMAIL LIST

Successful email marketing starts with a quality contact list. We'll discuss techniques for building and growing your email list organically while respecting permission and privacy guidelines to ensure your messages are received by an interested and engaged audience.

STRATEGIES FOR ENGAGEMENT AND CONVERSIONS

In this segment, we'll dive into strategies that can transform your emails from simple notifications to powerful conversion tools. These include personalizing messages, audience segmentation, responsive design, and creating valuable content that encourages recipients to open your emails and take action.

THE IMPORTANCE OF ONGOING RELATIONSHIPS

In addition to driving sales, email marketing is a great tool for nurturing relationships. Let's take a look at how you can use email to provide ongoing value, keep your brand top of mind, and build customer loyalty through consistent, relevant communications.

To optimize your email campaigns and ensure the best return on investment, it is essential to measure your success.

This chapter has reaffirmed email marketing as a powerful and versatile tool for achieving a variety of goals, from driving sales to building lasting customer relationships. The key to success lies in personalization, segmentation, and delivering valuable content that resonates with your audience.

Get ready now to enter the critical scenario of **"CRISIS MANAGEMENT AND ONLINE REPUTATION"** . In the next chapter, we will discover how communication strategies can be crucial to protect and restore your brand's reputation in the face of public challenges.

CRISIS MANAGEMENT AND ONLINE REPUTATION

As we enter the complex realms of digital communication, we are faced with the inevitable challenges of crisis management and protecting our online reputation. This chapter is dedicated to arming you with the strategies you need to navigate public image challenges, ensuring that your brand not only survives temporary storms, but emerges stronger.

UNDERSTANDING CRISIS MANAGEMENT

Crisis management involves preparing for and responding quickly and effectively to adverse events that could affect your brand's reputation. We'll explore the fundamentals of a robust crisis management plan, including identifying potential crises, assembling a response team, and creating a procedures manual.

COMMUNICATION STRATEGIES DURING A CRISIS

Communication is the cornerstone of effective crisis management. We will discuss how to develop key messages that are transparent, authentic, and empathetic, and how and when to distribute them to internal and external audiences. In addition, we will address the vital role of social media as both a monitoring and communication tool in times of crisis.

SAFEGUARDING ONLINE REPUTATION

Your brand's online reputation is a valuable asset, and it's especially vulnerable during crises. We'll look at techniques for monitoring and managing your digital presence, responding to negative feedback constructively, and proactively engaging with the online community to rebuild trust and credibility.

LEARNING FROM PAST CRISES

Every crisis offers a unique learning opportunity. We'll look at case studies of successful and unsuccessful crisis management, highlighting key lessons that can be applied to strengthen your prevention and response strategy.

Assessing the impact of a crisis and the success of recovery initiatives is essential for closure and continuous improvement.

This chapter has highlighted the critical importance of effective crisis management and protecting your online reputation for any brand in the digital environment. The strategies presented are designed to equip you with the knowledge to respond to crises effectively, minimizing damage and rebuilding public trust.

Get ready now to explore the valuable tool of **"CUSTOMER FEEDBACK AS A STRATEGIC TOOL"** in the next chapter. We will discover how to transform customer feedback from a potential source of crises into a powerful instrument for continuous improvement and innovation.

CUSTOMER FEEDBACK AS A STRATEGIC TOOL

As we delve deeper into our journey of valuing communication as an essential investment, we come to a fundamental aspect that can define a brand's long-term success: the strategic use of customer feedback. This chapter is dedicated to exploring how customer feedback, if leveraged well, can become an invaluable tool for learning, innovation, and continuous improvement.

THE IMPORTANCE OF CUSTOMER FEEDBACK

We begin with an overview of the intrinsic value of customer feedback. Each opinion offers a unique window into the experiences, needs and desires of your audience, acting as a guide for product adjustments, service improvements and optimization of communication strategies.

EFFICIENT FEEDBACK COLLECTION METHODS

Collecting feedback shouldn't be a passive process. We'll explore a variety of active and engaging techniques for collecting feedback, from online surveys and focus groups to social media sentiment analysis and post-interaction rating systems. We'll discuss how to implement these methods in a way that maximizes customer engagement and the quality of the information collected.

ANALYZING AND ACTING ON FEEDBACK

Collecting feedback is just the first step; the key is to analyze it properly and act on it. We'll cover strategies for categorizing and prioritizing feedback, identifying trends and patterns, and translating that information into concrete actions that improve product and service offerings and enrich the customer experience.

FEEDBACK AS A DRIVER OF INNOVATION

In addition to being a tool for continuous improvement, customer feedback can be a powerful catalyst for innovation. We'll discuss how customer insights can inspire new products, services, and market approaches, helping to keep your brand relevant and competitive.

Closing the feedback loop is key to building and maintaining customer trust. This segment is dedicated to best practices for communicating back to customers how their insights are being used, demonstrating the value your brand places on their opinions and reinforcing a positive long-term relationship.

This chapter has highlighted how customer feedback is not just an indicator of satisfaction, but a strategic lever for growth, innovation, and loyalty. By actively engaging with feedback, your brand can adapt, evolve, and thrive in a competitive marketplace.

Get ready now to move on to **"CROSS-PLATFORM COMMUNICATION STRATEGIES .**" In the next chapter, we'll explore how to integrate your communications cohesively and consistently across multiple channels to amplify impact and reinforce your brand identity.

MULTIPLATFORM COMMUNICATION STRATEGIES

As we continue our journey to maximize ROI in communications, we face the challenge of maintaining a cohesive and impactful message in a fragmented digital environment. This chapter is dedicated to uncovering how multiplatform communications strategies can reinforce your brand identity and optimize your reach and engagement across multiple channels.

THE NEED FOR MULTIPLATFORM COMMUNICATION

We begin with an overview of the importance of a multi-platform approach in the digital age. With audiences spread across multiple channels, from social media to email to websites, a unified strategy ensures that your message not only reaches but resonates with your target audience, no matter where they are.

DEVELOPING A COHESIVE MESSAGE

The key to effective cross-platform communication is cohesion. We'll explore how to develop a core message that can be adapted, but not diluted, across different platforms. This includes creating a consistent brand voice, recognizable visuals, and a central narrative that runs through all communications.

ADAPTABLE CONTENT STRATEGIES

We'll discuss how to create flexible content that can be customized to fit the unique needs of each platform, maximizing engagement and effectiveness. This involves understanding the nuances of each channel, from the ephemeral nature of Instagram Stories to the depth of LinkedIn articles, and tailoring your message to align with audience expectations on each.

INTEGRATION AND SYNCHRONIZATION BETWEEN PLATFORMS

A successful cross-platform strategy requires not only cohesive messaging, but also technical and temporal integration across channels. We'll cover techniques for synchronizing your campaigns, ensuring that product launches, major announcements, and other communications are orchestrated harmoniously across all touchpoints.

Evaluating the performance of your cross-platform strategy is critical to understanding what works and where adjustments are needed.

This chapter reinforced the importance of a strategic and integrated approach to multiplatform communication, essential to building a strong and cohesive brand presence in today's diverse digital environment.

Get ready now to enter the world of **"DATA ANALYSIS FOR DECISION MAKING"** . In the next chapter, we will explore how to use communication data analysis to inform more effective strategies, ensuring that your communication decisions are guided by accurate and impactful insights.

DATA ANALYSIS FOR DECISION MAKING

As we continue to explore the transformation of communications into a strategic investment for business growth and success, we are faced with a powerful tool in the digital age: data analytics. This chapter explores how the careful analysis of communications data can significantly improve decision-making, enabling communications strategies to be more aligned with audience needs and business goals.

FUNDAMENTALS OF DATA ANALYSIS IN COMMUNICATION

We'll introduce you to the basics of data analytics within the context of communications, explaining how data can be collected, interpreted and used to inform strategies. From social media engagement analytics to email opening patterns and website interactions, each data point provides valuable insights into audience behavior and preferences.

TOOLS AND TECHNOLOGIES FOR DATA ANALYSIS

With the vast amount of data available, choosing the right tools for collecting and analyzing it is crucial. Let's explore some of the most effective technologies and software for analyzing communications data, highlighting how they can be applied to gain actionable insights.

TRANSFORMING DATA INTO COMMUNICATION STRATEGIES

Data analysis goes beyond simply collecting information; it's about translating that data into tangible communication strategies. We'll discuss processes for identifying trends, audience behaviors, and content effectiveness, and how these findings can be used to adjust and refine your communication campaigns.

MEASURING SUCCESS AND ADJUSTING IN REAL TIME

One of the biggest benefits of data analytics is the ability to measure the success of your strategies in real time and make adjustments as needed. We'll look at how to set realistic KPIs (Key Performance Indicators), monitor campaign performance, and quickly adapt your approaches to optimize results.

While data analysis offers invaluable opportunities, it also faces challenges such as information overload and the need for specific skills to interpret data.

This chapter has highlighted data analytics as an essential backbone for effective strategic communications, enabling an informed and adaptive approach that can significantly improve the ROI of your communications initiatives.

Get ready now to explore **"CORPORATE SOCIAL RESPONSIBILITY"** in the next chapter. We'll discover how communicating your CSR initiatives can not only strengthen your brand reputation but also deeply engage your customers and stakeholders in a common cause.

CORPORATE SOCIAL RESPONSIBILITY

As we continue our journey to highlight communication as a vital investment for business success, we come to a point where ethics, business, and communication intersect: Corporate Social Responsibility (CSR). This chapter delves into the importance of integrating CSR into your brand's communication strategies, transforming good intentions into actions that not only benefit society, but also reinforce the positive perception and value of your brand.

WHAT IS CORPORATE SOCIAL RESPONSIBILITY?

CSR refers to business practices conducted in an ethical and sustainable manner that address social, environmental, and economic issues. We begin this chapter by defining CSR and discussing why it has become an expectation for modern businesses, not just a competitive differentiator.

INTEGRATING CSR INTO BRAND COMMUNICATION

We'll explore how effectively communicating your CSR initiatives can enhance your brand image, increase customer engagement, and attract talent who share your values. We'll discuss strategies for telling your CSR story authentically, ensuring your actions speak louder than your words and reflect your company's core values.

DEVELOPING IMPACTFUL CSR PROGRAMS

The key to a successful CSR program is alignment with your brand values and community needs. Let's look at how to identify CSR opportunities that resonate with your audience and how to implement programs that have a measurable impact on both society and your business.

MEASURING THE IMPACT OF CSR

Measuring the impact of your CSR initiatives is crucial to understanding their effectiveness and communicating that success to stakeholders. We'll cover the metrics and tools to assess the social, environmental, and economic impact of your CSR efforts, and how sharing those results can further strengthen your brand's reputation.

While CSR can be a powerful reputation booster, it also comes with its challenges, especially when perceived as disingenuous or merely promotional.

This chapter has reinforced corporate social responsibility as a fundamental pillar for building a strong, trusted and respected brand. By integrating CSR into your communications strategy, you can not only contribute positively to society but also create a deeper and more meaningful bond with your audience.

Get ready to delve into the realm of **"CORPORATE EVENTS AND PRODUCT LAUNCHES"** in the next chapter. We'll explore how to use events and launches to create memorable experiences that expand your brand's reach, reinforce your message, and drive engagement.

CORPORATE EVENTS AND PRODUCT LAUNCHES

As we continue our exploration of how to turn communications into a critical investment in brand growth, we come to the transformative potential of corporate events and product launches. This chapter focuses on the art of creating memorable experiences that not only capture your audience's attention, but also reinforce your brand message and drive engagement.

THE IMPORTANCE OF CORPORATE EVENTS AND PRODUCT LAUNCHES

We begin with an overview of the relevance of these events in modern marketing. Events and launches are unique opportunities to present your brand, products or services in a dynamic and interactive way, creating emotional connections with the public and generating media coverage.

PLANNING AND EXECUTING SUCCESSFUL EVENTS

The success of an event or launch depends on meticulous planning and flawless execution. We'll discuss the essential planning steps, from defining clear objectives and choosing the event format to logistics and scheduling. We'll also cover the importance of adapting events for virtual, hybrid, and in-person environments, taking into account current trends and audience preferences.

COMMUNICATING YOUR EVENT TO MAXIMIZE REACH

Effective communication is crucial to ensuring attendance and engagement at your event. We'll explore strategies for promoting your event or launch through a variety of channels, including social media, email marketing and influencer partnerships, ensuring your message reaches the desired audience.

ENGAGING THE PUBLIC BEFORE, DURING AND AFTER THE EVENT

Engaging your audience isn't limited to the day of the event. We'll look at techniques for building anticipation before the event, maximizing engagement during the event, and maintaining momentum after the event through exclusive content, social media interactions, and feedback opportunities.

Evaluating the impact of your event is essential to understanding its success and areas for improvement.

This chapter highlighted how corporate events and product launches can be powerful communication vehicles for your brand, creating unforgettable experiences that reinforce engagement and promote customer loyalty.

Get ready now to enter the field of **"INVESTMENT IN COMMUNICATION TECHNOLOGY"** in the next chapter. We will explore the latest trends and technological tools that can increase the effectiveness of your communication, ensuring that your brand stays ahead in an ever-evolving digital world.

INVESTMENT IN COMMUNICATION TECHNOLOGY

At this point in our journey to explore how to transform communications into a vital strategic investment, we turn our focus to the crucial role of emerging technologies in optimizing communications strategies. This chapter highlights the importance of investing in communications technology, exploring the tools and innovations that can enhance the reach and effectiveness of your brand's communications.

THE IMPORTANCE OF TECHNOLOGY IN MODERN COMMUNICATION

We introduce the chapter with an overview of how technology has transformed the communications landscape, enabling brands to connect with their audiences in ways that were previously unimaginable. We'll cover the rapid evolution of communications tools and the need for companies to stay up to date to avoid falling behind.

ESSENTIAL COMMUNICATION TOOLS FOR BRANDS

We'll explore a range of essential technologies and platforms that can enhance your brand's communications, from customer relationship management (CRM) systems and marketing automation platforms to advanced data analytics and artificial intelligence solutions. We'll discuss how these tools can be used to personalize communications, optimize campaigns, and improve the customer experience.

ADOPTING INNOVATIONS IN DIGITAL COMMUNICATION

With digital becoming increasingly prevalent, we'll be investigating the latest trends and innovations in digital communication, including augmented reality (AR), virtual reality (VR), chatbots and voice assistants. We'll examine how these technologies are redefining customer engagement and how they can be integrated into your communication strategy to create immersive and memorable experiences.

CHALLENGES AND CONSIDERATIONS IN THE

IMPLEMENTATION OF TECHNOLOGIES

Implementing new technologies comes with its own set of challenges, from cost and training issues to the need for cultural adaptation within the company. We will cover strategies to overcome these obstacles, ensuring a smooth transition and effective integration of technologies into your brand's communication.

To justify investment in communications technology, it is crucial to measure your return on investment (ROI).

This chapter has reinforced how strategic investment in communications technology can transform the way brands interact with their audiences, creating new opportunities for engagement, personalization, and impact. By embracing the latest innovations, your brand can stand out in a competitive marketplace and evolve with consumer expectations.

Get ready now to enter the field of **"NETWORKING AND STRATEGIC PARTNERSHIPS"** in the next chapter. We will explore how building networks and establishing strategic partnerships can be catalysts for brand growth and expanding the reach of your communication.

NETWORKING AND STRATEGIC PARTNERSHIPS

As we continue to explore the many facets of communication as a strategic investment for business success, we now look at the vital importance of networking and developing strategic partnerships. This chapter explores how cultivating professional relationships and alliances can significantly expand your brand's reach and influence, as well as generate mutually beneficial growth opportunities.

THE ART OF NETWORKING IN THE DIGITAL AGE

We begin by exploring the essence of networking in the modern context, highlighting its importance not only in face-to-face events but also in the vast digital world. We will discuss strategies for building and maintaining a professional network online, using platforms such as LinkedIn, virtual events and webinars, always keeping a focus on authenticity and mutual value.

DEVELOPING STRATEGIC PARTNERSHIPS

We'll dive into identifying and developing strategic partnerships that complement and strengthen your brand's goals. From co-branding and product collaborations to content partnerships and social responsibility initiatives, we'll explore how these alliances can create powerful synergies, expand your audience, and increase brand visibility.

STRATEGIES FOR EFFECTIVE NETWORKING

We'll cover practical techniques for effective networking, including the importance of offering value before expecting anything in return, the art of active listening, and the power of following through after the first few contacts. These strategies are designed to strengthen long-term professional connections that are essential for continued success.

MAXIMIZING THE IMPACT OF PARTNERSHIPS

We will explore how to maximize the impact of strategic partnerships through effective communication, alignment of goals, and collaborative project execution. We will discuss the importance of setting clear expectations, sharing resources, and jointly measuring success to ensure both parties fully benefit from the partnership.

Recognizing the challenges inherent in networking and partnership development, from misaligned goals to communication difficulties, we will offer solutions to overcome these obstacles. This includes strategies for resolving conflicts, renegotiating agreements, and, when necessary, terminating partnerships in an ethical and professional manner.

This chapter highlighted how effective networking and developing strategic partnerships are key to expanding your brand's reach and creating growth opportunities. By investing time and resources in these connections, your brand can reach new audiences, explore innovative markets, and strengthen its market position.

Get ready to dive into **"MULTICULTURAL AND GLOBAL COMMUNICATION"** in the next chapter. We'll explore how to adapt your communication strategies for global and multicultural markets, ensuring your message resonates with a diverse audience and further expanding your brand's impact worldwide.

MULTICULTURAL AND GLOBAL COMMUNICATION

Navigating the intricate world of corporate communications, we recognize the growing importance of addressing global and multicultural audiences with sensitivity and effectiveness. This chapter explores strategies for adapting your brand communications to different cultures and regions, ensuring that your message is not only heard, but also respected and valued in a global context.

UNDERSTANDING MULTICULTURAL COMMUNICATION

We begin by outlining the global communications landscape, emphasizing the need to understand the cultural nuances that influence consumer perception and behavior. We will discuss the importance of in-depth cultural research and empathy to create messages that resonate with diverse audiences, avoiding stereotypes and misunderstandings.

DEVELOPING GLOBAL COMMUNICATION STRATEGIES

We will cover how to develop communications strategies that are truly global, considering not only language translation but also content transcription , ensuring that context, tone and intent are appropriate and effective across cultures. We will explore the importance of adapting marketing and communications approaches to meet local expectations and norms.

TOOLS AND TECHNOLOGIES FOR GLOBAL COMMUNICATION

We'll look at the tools and technologies that can facilitate effective communication in a global context, from project management and translation platforms to data analytics solutions that help you better understand international audiences. We'll discuss how these tools can help you coordinate multicultural campaigns and monitor their success.

SUCCESS STORIES AND LESSONS LEARNED

We will illustrate this chapter with case studies of brands that have achieved significant success in global markets, analyzing the strategies they employed and the lessons learned along the way. These examples will serve as inspiration and guidance for brands aspiring to expand their global presence.

Recognizing the challenges of communicating on a multicultural stage, we will discuss how to navigate cultural sensitivities and avoid faux pas that can harm brand image.

This chapter has highlighted the importance of a thoughtful and informed approach to multicultural and global communication, essential for brands seeking to build a strong and respected international presence.

Get ready to dive into the analysis of **"PAID ADVERTISING: EVALUATING ROI"** in the next chapter. We'll explore how to navigate the complex world of paid advertising across multiple channels, maximizing return on investment and achieving strategic communication goals.

PAID ADVERTISING: EVALUATING ROI

As we delve deeper into the nuances of corporate communications as a strategic investment, we come to the complexities of paid advertising and its critical role in expanding brand reach and converting interest into tangible action. This chapter explores the facets of paid advertising across platforms, focusing on how to assess and maximize return on investment (ROI) to ensure that every dollar invested contributes meaningfully to brand growth objectives.

INTRODUCTION TO PAID ADVERTISING

We'll start with an overview of paid advertising, including its many formats, from social media and search engine ads to website banners and beyond. We'll cover the importance of selecting the channels that best align with your brand's goals and target audience to ensure that paid advertising is an effective investment, not just a cost.

DEFINING AND MEASURING ROI IN PAID ADVERTISING

Evaluating the success of paid advertising requires a clear understanding of how to measure ROI. We'll discuss methods for setting clear, measurable goals, tracking conversions, and evaluating performance relative to initial investment. This includes analyzing key metrics such as cost per acquisition (CPA), customer lifetime value (LTV), and conversion rate.

STRATEGIES TO MAXIMIZE ROI

With the paid advertising landscape becoming increasingly competitive, optimizing your campaigns is essential. We'll explore advanced strategies, from ad targeting and personalization to landing page optimization. pages and A/B testing. Plus, we'll discuss the importance of creativity and innovation in ad design and messaging to stand out from the crowd.

BUDGET MANAGEMENT AND RESOURCE ALLOCATION

Effectively managing your advertising budget is crucial to avoiding waste and maximizing impact. We'll cover techniques for intelligently allocating resources across different platforms and campaigns, adjusting your investment based on performance and market changes to ensure efficient ad spend.

Paid advertising faces several challenges, from market saturation to changes in platform policies and consumer perception.

This chapter has highlighted paid advertising as a crucial element of any brand's communications strategy, with a particular focus on measuring and optimizing ROI. By investing wisely and monitoring performance closely, brands can ensure that their paid advertising contributes significantly to their business and communications objectives.

Get ready now to explore **"NONVERBAL COMMUNICATION AND ITS IMPORTANCE"** in the next chapter. We will dive into the subtleties of nonverbal communication, addressing how aspects such as design, color and presence can influence brand perception and customer engagement, complementing and enhancing your overall communication.

NONVERBAL COMMUNICATION AND ITS IMPORTANCE

In our ongoing journey to highlight all aspects of communication as essential investments for brand success, we now delve into the dimension of nonverbal communication. This chapter explores how visual, gestural and spatial elements can convey powerful messages about your brand, influencing consumer perceptions and behaviors without the need for words.

UNDERSTANDING NONVERBAL COMMUNICATION

We begin with an introduction to nonverbal communication, highlighting its ability to convey emotions, values and brand identity. We will cover the various elements of nonverbal communication, including body language, design, color, typography and imagery, and how they can be strategically used in a brand's interactions with its audience.

DESIGN AND COLOR: THE PSYCHOLOGY BEHIND THE CHOICE

We'll delve into the psychology of color and visual design, explaining how different colors and design styles can evoke specific emotions and communicate subliminal brand messages. We'll discuss how to align color choices and design with your brand message and values to reinforce your visual identity and appeal to your target audience.

THE INFLUENCE OF SPACE AND ARCHITECTURE

We'll explore the importance of physical space and architecture, especially for brands with a retail or corporate presence. We'll examine how the layout of space, interior design, and customer experience in the physical environment can enhance brand communication and improve consumer perception.

THE POWER OF IMAGES AND BODY LANGUAGE

Imagery and body language in marketing materials, including photographs, videos, and visual representations of your brand's team, are also crucial forms of nonverbal communication. We'll discuss how to use authentic imagery and positive body language to build trust and create an emotional connection with your audience.

We will bring all of these elements together into a cohesive strategy, showing how nonverbal communication can be integrated into marketing and brand communications campaigns to complement and reinforce verbal messages, creating a rich and engaging brand experience.

This chapter has illustrated how nonverbal communication is an essential component of brand expression, providing an additional layer of meaning and emotion to interactions with audiences. By carefully selecting and integrating visual and spatial elements, brands can deepen engagement and strengthen brand identity.

Get ready to enter the world of **"THE PODCAST AGE: HARNESSING NEW CHANNELS"** in the next chapter. We'll explore how podcasts have become an influential communication tool for brands, allowing them to tell stories, share knowledge, and connect with audiences in unique and personal ways.

THE PODCAST ERA: HAVING ADVANTAGE OF NEW CHANNELS

As we continue to explore the broad spectrum of communication as a strategic investment, we turn to an increasingly popular and personal means of connecting with audiences around the world: podcasts. This chapter delves into the power of podcasts as a dynamic tool for brands to share stories, insights, and values, establishing a deep and authentic connection with listeners.

INTRODUCTION TO PODCASTS IN BRAND COMMUNICATION

We'll begin by examining the rise of podcasting as a medium and its growing importance in the digital marketing mix . We'll discuss the unique appeal of podcasts, including their ability to engage listeners through rich, immersive content that's available for on - the -go consumption.

DEVELOPING COMPELLING CONTENT FOR PODCASTS

We'll cover the essence of creating a captivating podcast, focusing on the importance of relevant, engaging content that resonates with your target audience. We'll discuss strategies for planning episodes, choosing relevant topics, and creating a content calendar that keeps listeners engaged and eager for more.

TECHNIQUES TO MAXIMIZE REACH AND ENGAGEMENT

We'll explore techniques for promoting your podcast and expanding its reach, including search engine optimization (SEO), social media marketing, strategic partnerships with other podcasters , and participation in podcast platforms and directories. We'll also cover how to encourage listener engagement and participation by building an active community around your podcast.

MEASURING THE SUCCESS OF YOUR PODCAST

Measuring the impact of your podcast is crucial to understanding its success and guiding future strategies. We'll discuss key performance metrics, including downloads, listener engagement, and social shares, and how to use this information to continually adjust and improve your content and approach.

We'll acknowledge the challenges faced in creating and distributing podcasts, from ensuring high-quality production to building a loyal audience.

This chapter has highlighted podcasts as a valuable and impactful form of brand communication that can build deep and lasting connections with global audiences. Through authentic and engaging content, podcasts offer a unique platform to tell your brand's story in an intimate and memorable way.

Get ready now to enter the realm of **"SUSTAINABILITY IN COMMUNICATION"** in the next chapter. We will discuss how integrating sustainability principles into your communication can not only reinforce your brand's commitment to ethical and responsible practices, but also resonate with consumers who are increasingly aware of environmental and social issues.

SUSTAINABILITY IN COMMUNICATION

As we explore the many aspects that make communication a crucial strategic investment, we turn our attention to a topic of growing importance and relevance: sustainability. This chapter focuses on how to effectively incorporate and communicate a brand's sustainability practices, reinforcing not only its commitment to the future of the planet, but also aligning with the expectations of an increasingly conscious audience.

THE ROLE OF SUSTAINABILITY IN BRAND COMMUNICATION

We will begin with an overview of the importance of sustainability in the current context, highlighting how sustainable practices have become a key criterion for consumers when choosing brands and products. We will discuss the positive impact that effective communication of sustainability initiatives can have on brand perception and customer loyalty.

CREATING A SUSTAINABLE COMMUNICATION STRATEGY

We'll explore approaches to developing a communications strategy that authentically reflects a brand's commitment to sustainability. This includes tips for ensuring that communications are transparent, actionable, and avoid "greenwashing." We'll emphasize the importance of stories and narratives that demonstrate real impact, rather than simply making unsubstantiated claims.

METRICS AND TOOLS FOR SUSTAINABILITY COMMUNICATION

We'll cover how to measure and communicate the impact of sustainability initiatives in a way that's understandable and meaningful to your audience. We'll discuss tools and certifications that can help validate your brand's sustainability efforts, as well as metrics to track progress toward sustainability goals.

INVOLVING STAKEHOLDERS IN THE SUSTAINABILITY JOURNEY

Sustainability communication goes beyond consumers to investors, partners and communities. We will explore strategies to engage all stakeholders in the brand's sustainability journey, encouraging collaboration and support for broader initiatives that benefit both the business and the environment.

Recognizing the challenges associated with effectively communicating sustainable practices, we will address how to address public skepticism, regulatory barriers, and internal limitations.

This chapter highlighted the critical importance of integrating sustainability into communication strategies, reinforcing the brand's commitment to responsible practices and building an authentic connection with conscious consumers.

Get ready now to move on to **"MEASURING COMMUNICATIONS IMPACT"** in the next chapter. We'll explore the essential methodologies and tools for evaluating the effectiveness of your communications strategies, ensuring that each message, campaign and initiative positively contributes to your brand's overall goals.

MEASURING THE IMPACT OF COMMUNICATION

As we explore the depth and breadth of communications as a strategic investment, we come to a critical aspect of ensuring the long-term success of any strategy: measuring its impact. This chapter is dedicated to uncovering the essential practices, tools, and methodologies for evaluating the effectiveness of communications initiatives, enabling brands to make informed adjustments to optimize return on investment.

THE IMPORTANCE OF MEASUREMENT IN COMMUNICATION

We'll start by discussing why measurement is crucial in the context of corporate communications. Being able to quantify the success of your communications strategies not only validates the investment made, but also provides valuable insights for future improvements, ensuring that your brand messages continue to resonate with your target audience.

DEFINING RELEVANT METRICS AND KPIS

An effective approach to measurement starts with defining clear and relevant metrics and KPIs (Key Performance Indicators). Let's explore how to select these indicators based on your specific communication goals, from increasing brand awareness to converting sales and building customer loyalty.

TOOLS AND TECHNOLOGIES FOR DATA COLLECTION

With the vast array of tools and technologies available, choosing the right ones to collect and analyze data can be challenging. We'll cover the most effective options on the market, from social media analytics software to advanced CRM and website analytics platforms, highlighting how they can be used to gather actionable insights.

ANALYZING DATA TO INFORM FUTURE STRATEGIES

Analyzing collected data is where true insights are discovered. We will discuss methodologies for effectively interpreting data, identifying trends and patterns, and how these findings can be used to refine and adjust communication strategies, ensuring they remain aligned with evolving audience expectations and behaviors.

OVERCOMING CHALLENGES IN MEASURING IMPACT

Measuring the impact of communications faces a number of challenges, from direct attribution of results to assessing brand perception and sentiment. We'll explore strategies to overcome these obstacles, ensuring an accurate assessment of your communications performance.

We've completed our comprehensive and in-depth journey on how to transform communication into a strategic investment for brands, covering everything from the fundamentals of effective communication to advanced strategies and inspiring success stories. It's now essential to recognize that while this book provides a solid foundation and valuable insights, the communications landscape is always evolving. Brands must remain agile, innovative and, above all, committed to authentically connecting with their audiences.

CONTINUING YOUR COMMUNICATION JOURNEY

As you move forward, remember that communications is a dynamic field, driven by both technological advances and changing consumer preferences and behaviors. Stay informed about the latest trends, tools, and best practices. Never underestimate the power of listening to your audience, as direct feedback can be one of the richest sources of insight and inspiration.

THE IMPORTANCE OF ADAPTABILITY

Success in communications comes not only from meticulously planning, but also from being able to adapt quickly. Be prepared to review and adjust your strategies based on performance, feedback, and changes in the market environment. Adaptability is key to staying relevant and continuing to grow in a competitive market.

CONTINUOUS INVESTMENT IN LEARNING

Ongoing education is crucial. Consider attending workshops, seminars, and conferences, as well as engaging in professional networks where you can share experiences and learn from your peers. Investing in ongoing learning ensures that you and your team remain at the forefront of communications innovation.

BUILDING FOR THE FUTURE

As you build the future of communication for your brand, remember that every interaction counts. Be consistent in your efforts, maintain integrity in your message, and always aim to create genuine value for your audience. Effective communication is a continuous cycle of learning, adapting, and growing.

We hope this book has served as a valuable resource and practical guide to transforming your brand's communications. Remember, the communications journey is an ongoing one, with each chapter of your brand story offering the opportunity to engage, inspire, and connect in new and meaningful ways.

As we conclude this detailed journey, we encourage you to take forward the lessons learned, apply the strategies discussed, and continue exploring new ways to communicate your brand's unique essence to the world. Communication is truly an investment that, when done carefully and strategically, yields incalculable returns.

END OF THE JOURNEY, BUT NOT OF THE STORY

Completing this book does not mark the end, but rather a new beginning. With the tools, knowledge, and strategies we've shared, you are now better prepared than ever to write the next chapters of your communications story. Continue to strive for excellence, innovate, and make communications a driving force behind your brand's success. The future is bright, and we look forward to seeing where your communications journey takes you.

As we turn the final page of this journey together, I sincerely hope that the lessons shared here have touched your heart and opened up new perspectives. If this book has brought you any value, I kindly ask that you take a moment to leave a review on Amazon. Your words not only help me grow and improve my craft, but they also guide other readers in their quest for knowledge and inspiration. Your feedback is a valuable gift, both to me and to the community of readers seeking transformative stories. I sincerely thank you for sharing this journey with me, and I hope we can meet again in the pages of a new adventure.

REGINALDO OSNILDO

Hello, I'm Reginaldo Osnildo, an author and innovator in the areas of sales, technology, and communication strategies. My experience ranges from academia, as a professor and researcher at the University of Southern Santa Catarina, to practice as a strategist at Grupo Catarinense de Rádios. With a PhD in sales narratives and digital convergence, and a master's degree in storytelling and social imaginary, I bring to my readers a unique fusion of theory and practice. My goal is to provide knowledge in simple, practical, and didactic language, encouraging direct application in personal and professional life.

Yours sincerely

Reginaldo Osnildo

+55 48 991913865

reginaldoosnildo@gmail.com

www.ingramcontent.com/pod-product-compliance
Lightning Source LLC
Chambersburg PA
CBHW070352230526
45471CB00006B/2526